Key Stage **2**

Schofield & Sims

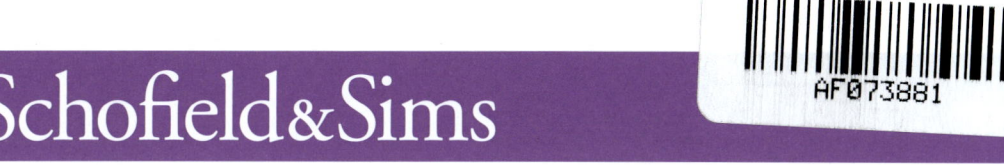

Fractions 3

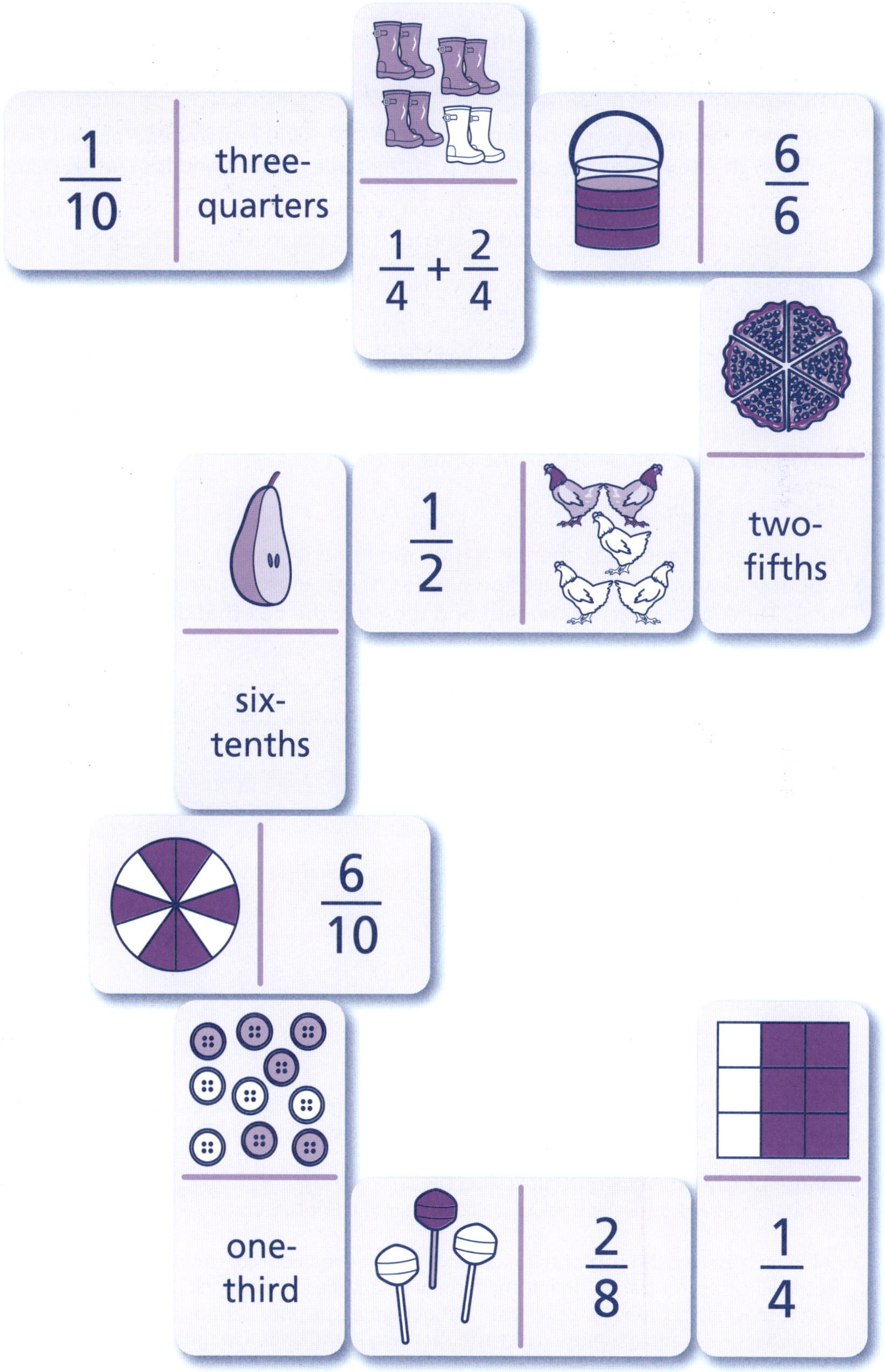

Name ______________________

Introduction

Welcome to this book

This book will help you learn about fractions, decimals and percentages. These are used every day when we want to describe parts of things. This will help with your overall maths learning.

This book is divided into units with three sections of questions in each unit. Start at the beginning and work your way through the book, building up your knowledge and skills.

Finding your way around

Each unit has an important point for you to learn and remember. You will find this learning point in the **Key point** box at the top of the page. Read it and look at the example.

The first section of questions in each unit is called **Get started**. These are straightforward, quick questions that are related to the learning objective.

The next section of questions is called **Now try these**. These are number and practical problems that take the topic further.

The final section of questions is called **Challenge**. These are problem-solving questions involving a greater level of challenge.

There are three **Check-up tests** in this book. There is also a **Final test** which you should take when you have completed all the units.

Checking progress

At the back of the book there is a **How did I find it?** chart. You can use this to help you think about your learning. You will find a series of statements relating to the key points in each unit. Think about each statement and then tick the box that describes how you feel about it – **difficult**, **getting there** or **easy**.

There is also a **Glossary** at the back of this book, where you can look up the meaning of important mathematical words that you will come across.

Published by **Schofield & Sims Ltd**, 7 Mariner Court, Wakefield, West Yorkshire WF4 3FL, UK
Telephone 01484 607080
www.schofieldandsims.co.uk

This edition copyright © Schofield & Sims Ltd, 2017
First published in 2017
Ninth impression 2025

Authors: **Hilary Koll and Steve Mills**
Hilary Koll and Steve Mills have asserted their moral rights under the Copyright, Designs and Patents Act, 1988, to be identified as the authors of this work.

British Library Cataloguing in Publication Data
A catalogue record for this book is available from the British Library.

All rights reserved. No part of this publication may be reproduced, stored in a retrieval system, or transmitted in any form or by any means, electronic, mechanical, photocopying, recording or otherwise, without either the prior permission of the publisher or a licence permitting restricted copying in the United Kingdom issued by the Copyright Licensing Agency Ltd.

Design by **Oxford Designers & Illustrators Ltd**
Printed in the UK by **Page Bros (Norwich) Ltd**

ISBN 978 07217 1379 3

Contents

Unit 1	Recognise quarters as fractions of shapes	4
Unit 2	Recognise halves and quarters of sets	6
Unit 3	Count up and down in halves and quarters	8
Unit 4	Understand fractions with the numerator 1	10
Unit 5	Compare fractions with the numerator 1	12
Unit 6	Recognise unit fractions as a division of a quantity	14
	Check-up test 1	16
Unit 7	Understand non-unit fractions as areas of shapes	18
Unit 8	Recognise tenths and count in tenths	20
Unit 9	Recognise that tenths arise from dividing by 10	22
Unit 10	Use fractions as numbers on a number line	24
Unit 11	Compare fractions with the same denominator	26
Unit 12	Recognise fractions of a set of objects	28
	Check-up test 2	30
Unit 13	Use non-unit fractions in a variety of representations	32
Unit 14	Recognise fractions showing the same amount	34
Unit 15	Find equivalent fractions using a fraction wall	36
Unit 16	Add fractions with the same denominator	38
Unit 17	Subtract fractions with the same denominator	40
Unit 18	Solve problems with measures	42
	Check-up test 3	44
	Final test	46
	How did I find it?	50
	Glossary	51

UNIT 1 Recognise quarters as fractions of shapes

Key point

$\frac{1}{4}$ is the same as **one-quarter**.

numerator ⟶ 1
denominator ⟶ 4

The **4** on the bottom of the fraction (the **denominator**) shows **how many equal parts a whole is split into**.

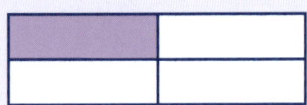

$\frac{1}{4}$ of this shape is purple. **1** out of **4 equal parts** is purple.

Get started

1 True or false? $\frac{1}{4}$ of the shape is purple.

a) 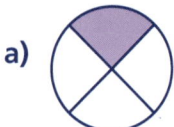 True ☐ False ☐

b)  True ☐ False ☐

2 What fraction of this shape is purple?
_____

3 Write the denominator of one-quarter. _____

4 Write the numerator of one-quarter. _____

5 True or false? One-quarter is purple.

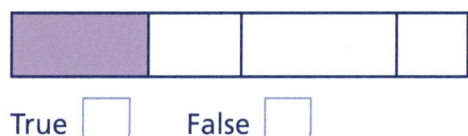

True ☐ False ☐

6 Tick the shape with $\frac{1}{4}$ shaded.

7 How many equal parts is a shape divided into to show quarters?
_____

8 Write $\frac{1}{4}$ in words.
_____

Now try these

9 Tick the two shapes which have $\frac{1}{4}$ shaded.

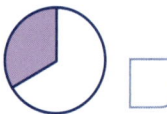 ☐  ☐  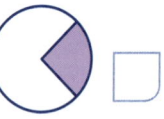 ☐  ☐

10 True or false? $\frac{1}{4}$ is half of $\frac{1}{2}$. True ☐ False ☐

11 How many quarters make a half? _____ quarters

12 How many people can each have $\frac{1}{4}$ of Jo's birthday cake? _____

Schofield & Sims Fractions, Decimals and Percentages Fractions 3

13) What number will the arrow point to after a $\frac{1}{4}$ turn clockwise? _____

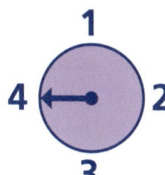

14) Write one-quarter as a fraction. _____

15) True or false? $\frac{1}{4} + \frac{1}{4} = \frac{1}{2}$ True ☐   False ☐

16) What fraction of this shape is purple? _____

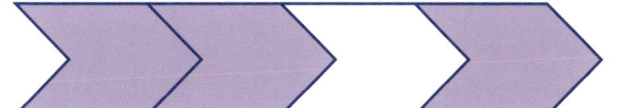

Challenge

17) What number does the minute hand of a clock point to at 'quarter past'? _____

18) What number does the minute hand of a clock point to at 'quarter to'? _____

19) A pizza is cut into four equal slices. What fraction of the whole pizza is one slice? _____

20) $\frac{1}{4}$ litre is poured into this empty 1 litre container. Which letter will the liquid reach? _____

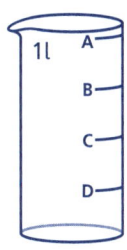

21) A chocolate bar has 8 chunks. Sam eats one-quarter of the bar. How many chunks does he eat? _____

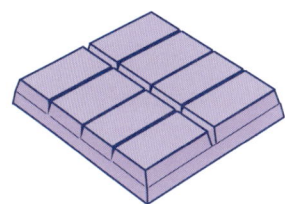

22) A 1m plank of wood is cut into four equal lengths. What fraction of a metre are three of these lengths together? _____ m

23) Joshua spent $\frac{1}{2}$ hour eating the main course of his meal and $\frac{1}{4}$ hour eating dessert.

   a) What fraction of an hour did he spend eating altogether? _____ hr

   b) How many minutes is this? _____ min

24) The dial on a washing machine has 8 settings. The arrow is pointing to 4. What number will it point to after a quarter turn clockwise? _____

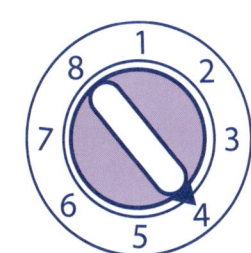

5

UNIT 2 Recognise halves and quarters of sets

Key point

Fractions can be used to show the parts of **sets of objects**.
These cards are sorted into 4 equal-sized groups.

 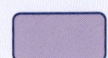    

This shows that $\frac{1}{4}$ of the cards are purple and $\frac{3}{4}$ of the cards are white.

There are 8 cards so $\frac{1}{4}$ of 8 cards = 2 cards and $\frac{3}{4}$ of 8 cards = 6 cards.

Get started

1 Colour $\frac{1}{4}$ of this set of cubes.

2 What fraction of the ants are on the leaf? _____

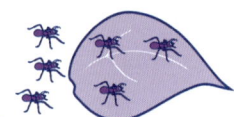

3 Tick more squares so that half the squares in this grid are ticked.

4 What fraction of the horses are wearing saddles? _____

5 A bus has 12 children on it. Six are girls. What fraction are girls?

_____

6 Find one-quarter of 16.

_____

7 Write the missing number.

$\frac{1}{\boxed{}}$ of 20 sweets is 10 sweets.

8 What fraction of these marbles are purple?

_____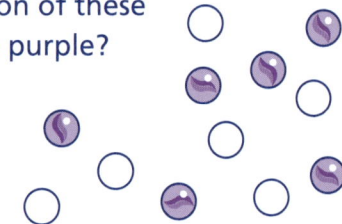

Now try these

9 What fraction of the grid is: a) purple? _____

b) white? _____

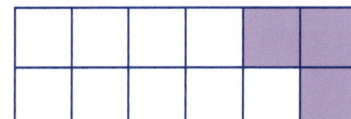

10 There are six steps. Aisha is on the third step.
What fraction of the way up the steps is she? _____

11 True or false? Harry ate 2 of the 8 cupcakes in a box.
He has eaten one-quarter of them.   True ☐   False ☐

12 Tick the tile pattern which shows $\frac{1}{4}$ purple.

13 Leah pours 8 cups of juice. 2 cups have orange juice. The rest have apple juice. What fraction of the cups have apple juice? _____

14 Ethan has 8 pound coins. He spends half of them. How much money has he now? £_____

15 A bag contains 6 red apples, 3 yellow apples and 3 green apples.

What fraction of the apples are: a) red? _____ b) green? _____

16 A small wall is made from 14 bricks in a row. How many bricks in half a row? _____

Challenge

17 A book has 20 pages. Ali has read 5 pages. What fraction of the book has Ali read? _____

18 Yusuf works for 21 of the 28 days in February.
What fraction of the days in February does Yusuf not work? _____

19 Three-quarters of the beads
on a necklace are silver.
How many beads are silver? _____

20 There are 18 sweets in half a packet of sweets.
How many sweets are there in a quarter of a packet? _____

21 How many minutes in:

a) half an hour? _____ min

b) one-quarter of an hour? _____ min

c) three-quarters of an hour? _____ min

22 Alice has one pound in 1p coins. She sorts the coins into four equal piles.
What is the value of the coins in one pile? _____ p

23 A tennis club has 40 children. $\frac{1}{4}$ of them are boys. How many are girls? _____

24 Four teams play in a tournament. Two of the teams wear red.
Write two different fractions to show what fraction of the teams wear red. _____ or _____

7

UNIT 3 Count up and down in halves and quarters

Key point

When counting in halves from 0, every other number is a whole number:

0, $\frac{1}{2}$, 1, $1\frac{1}{2}$, 2, $2\frac{1}{2}$, 3 …

When counting in quarters from 0 remember $\frac{2}{4}$ and $\frac{1}{2}$ have the same value:

0, $\frac{1}{4}$, $\frac{2}{4}$, $\frac{3}{4}$, 1, $1\frac{1}{4}$, $1\frac{2}{4}$, $1\frac{3}{4}$, 2, $2\frac{1}{4}$, $2\frac{2}{4}$, $2\frac{3}{4}$, 3 …

Both are correct.

0, $\frac{1}{4}$, $\frac{1}{2}$, $\frac{3}{4}$, 1, $1\frac{1}{4}$, $1\frac{1}{2}$, $1\frac{3}{4}$, 2, $2\frac{1}{4}$, $2\frac{1}{2}$, $2\frac{3}{4}$, 3 …

Get started

1 How many faces are purple?

_____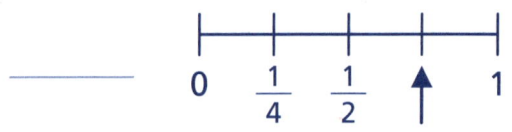

2 What number is the arrow pointing to?

_____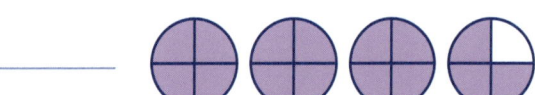

3 What is one-quarter more than $2\frac{1}{2}$?

_____

4 What is one-quarter less than four wholes?

_____

5 Write the missing number in this sequence.

0, $\frac{1}{2}$, 1, $1\frac{1}{2}$, _____, $2\frac{1}{2}$

6 What is $\frac{1}{4}$ more than $1\frac{1}{4}$?

_____

7 Write the next number in the sequence.

3, $3\frac{1}{4}$, $3\frac{1}{2}$, $3\frac{3}{4}$, 4, _____

8 What are eight halves? _____ wholes

Now try these

9 When counting on in halves, what number comes after 3? _____

10 What is $1\frac{3}{4} + \frac{1}{4}$? _____

11 Write the next two numbers in this sequence. $7\frac{1}{2}$, $7\frac{1}{4}$, 7, $6\frac{3}{4}$, $6\frac{1}{2}$, _____ , _____

12 How many quarters are in $2\frac{1}{2}$? _____ quarters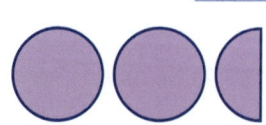

13 How many halves in six wholes? _____ halves

14 How heavy is the pumpkin?

_____ kg

15 Look at the number line. Write the values of A and B.   A = _____   B = _____

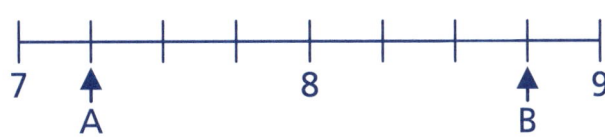

16 Count back ten-quarters from 5. What number do you reach? _____

Challenge

17 Lucy counts on an even number of halves from 0. Circle the number she finishes on.

$5\frac{1}{2}$ $6\frac{1}{4}$ 3 $3\frac{3}{4}$ $4\frac{1}{2}$

18 Each of Eva's steps is half a metre apart when she walks.

If she takes 9 steps, how far has she walked? _____ m

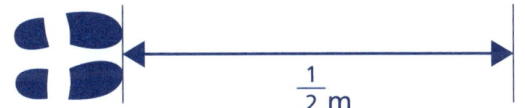

19 What number is two-quarters more than $4\frac{3}{4}$? _____

20 What is $7\frac{1}{2} - \frac{3}{4}$? _____

21 A fountain pours $\frac{1}{4}$ litre of water every second.
How much water will it pour in 11 seconds? _____ l

22 Jack is at the cinema. The adverts last $\frac{1}{2}$ hour and the film lasts $1\frac{3}{4}$ hours.
How long does he watch these in total?

_____ hr

23 Amir weighs $20\frac{1}{2}$ kg. Chloe weighs $3\frac{3}{4}$ kg less. How much does Chloe weigh? _____ kg

24 How many quarters greater than $8\frac{1}{2}$ is 10? _____ quarters

UNIT 4 Understand fractions with the numerator 1

Key point

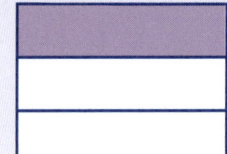 $\frac{1}{3}$ is one-third.   The **3** on the bottom of the fraction (the **denominator**) shows **how many equal parts a whole is split into**.

To find the **denominator**, see how many equal parts the whole is split into. If a whole is split into **3** equal parts, each part is $\frac{1}{3}$ (one-third). If it is split into **5** equal parts each part is $\frac{1}{5}$ (one-fifth) and so on.

Get started

1 How many equal parts has this shape been divided into?

_____

2 Tick the square that is $\frac{1}{3}$ purple.

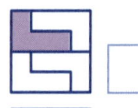 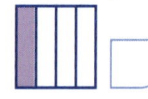 

3 Colour one-fifth of this star.

4 A cake is cut into 8 equal slices. What fraction of the cake is 1 slice? _____

5 What fraction of this pizza is each slice?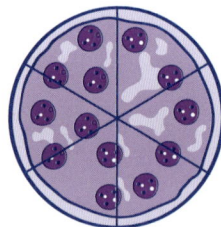

_____

6 Ben scored 1 out of 5 points in a quiz. Write this as a fraction.

_____

7 How many ninths make up one whole?

_____ ninths

8 A chocolate bar has five equal-sized chunks. Write in words what fraction of the bar is one chunk.

_____

Now try these

9 Tick the circle that has about $\frac{1}{3}$ shaded.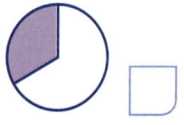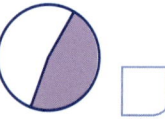

10 A melon is cut into seven equal slices. What fraction of the melon is one slice? _____

11 How many eighths make: **a)** a whole? _____ eighths   **b)** a half? _____ eighths

12 How many people can each have a sixth of Sara's birthday cake? _____

13 What fraction of these beads are white? _____

14 True or false? One-fifth of this shape is purple.
True ☐   False ☐

15 What fraction of this shape is not purple?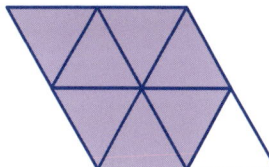

_____

16 What fraction of this cuboid is each cube? Write the fraction in words.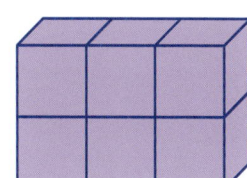

_____

Challenge

17 A tabletop is covered in tiles. Eight tiles are white and one is green. What fraction of the tiles are green? _____

18 A 1m stick is cut into five equal lengths. What fraction of a metre is each length? _____ m

19 One-quarter of an hour is 15 minutes.
How many minutes is one-third of an hour?

_____ min

20 The dial on a dishwasher has 8 settings. The arrow points to 6.
What will it point to after an eighth of a turn clockwise? _____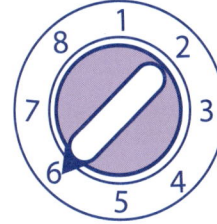

21 Isaac pours one cup of apple juice and four cups of orange juice into a jug. What fraction of the mixture is apple juice? _____

22 The minute hand of a clock moves from 12 to 1.
What fraction of the clock face has the hand moved? _____

23 If one whole is divided by 3, what fraction do you get?

$1 \div 3 = \dfrac{\boxed{}}{3}$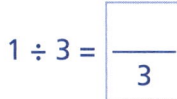

24 Amy makes a hanging decoration using only paper pentagons of the same size. She uses 5 red, 2 gold and 1 silver pentagon.
What fraction of the decoration is: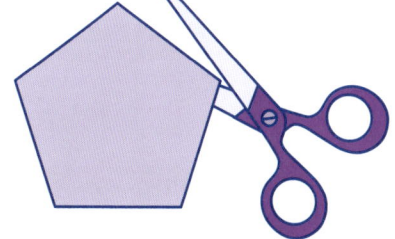

a) silver? _____   b) not silver? _____

UNIT 5 Compare fractions with the numerator 1

Key point

The **denominator** shows **how many equal parts a whole is split into**.

The **more parts** the whole is split into, the **smaller** each part is.

For fractions with the **numerator 1**, the **larger** the **denominator** the **smaller** the **value of the fraction**.

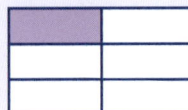 $\frac{1}{6}$ is smaller than $\frac{1}{4}$.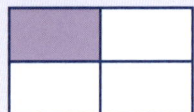

$$\frac{1}{6} < \frac{1}{4}$$

Get started

1 True or false? $\frac{1}{4}$ is larger than $\frac{1}{2}$.

True ☐   False ☐

2 Write in words the name of the larger fraction shown.

_____

3 Write in digits the smaller fraction shown.

_____

4 True or false? $\frac{1}{3}$ is greater than $\frac{1}{2}$.

True ☐   False ☐

5 Which makes larger slices?

A pie cut into 4 slices. ☐

The same pie cut into 5 slices. ☐

6 Circle the fraction that is smaller than one-quarter. $\frac{1}{3}$ $\frac{1}{2}$ $\frac{1}{5}$

7 True or false? $\frac{1}{3} < \frac{1}{2}$

True ☐   False ☐

8 Use either the < or > sign to show which is larger.

$\frac{1}{6}$ ☐ $\frac{1}{4}$

Now try these

9 Is one-eighth of a kilogram more or less than one-quarter of a kilogram? _____

10 Tick to show how the fractions in this sequence are ordered: $\frac{1}{2}, \frac{1}{3}, \frac{1}{4}, \frac{1}{5}, \frac{1}{6}$

smallest to largest ☐   largest to smallest ☐

11 Which letter on the number line shows:

a) $\frac{1}{2}$? _____   b) $\frac{1}{8}$? _____

c) Which of the two fractions is larger? _____

12 Two jugs are the same size. Jug A is $\frac{1}{8}$ full. Jug B is $\frac{1}{6}$ full. Which jug contains more? _____

13 Tick the longer time. $\frac{1}{6}$ of an hour ☐ $\frac{1}{2}$ an hour ☐

14 Write these fractions from smallest to largest:
$\frac{1}{7}$ $\frac{1}{3}$ $\frac{1}{9}$ _____ _____ _____

15 Callum has a box of chocolates. He gives $\frac{1}{4}$ to Sam and $\frac{1}{6}$ to Li.

Who gets more chocolates – Sam or Li? _____

16 Write these fractions from smallest to largest:
$\frac{1}{4}$ $\frac{1}{2}$ $\frac{1}{8}$ $\frac{1}{6}$ _____ _____ _____ _____

Challenge

17 Alfie cuts two pizzas of the same size into slices. He cuts one into fifths and the other into sixths. Alfie eats one of the smaller slices. What fraction of a whole pizza does he eat? _____

18 What is the missing number if this fraction is larger than one-fifth but smaller than one-third? $\frac{1}{\Box}$

19 Emma walked for one-quarter of a kilometre. Rosie walked for one-sixth of a kilometre. Who walked further? _____

20 Draw ticks on one-eighth of this grid and crosses on one-sixth. Are there more squares with ticks or crosses? _____

21 Cross out one of these fractions so that the rest are in order of size: $\frac{1}{6}$ $\frac{1}{4}$ $\frac{1}{3}$ $\frac{1}{5}$ $\frac{1}{2}$

22 On this jug, which letter shows:

a) $\frac{1}{4}$ of a litre? _____

b) $\frac{1}{5}$ of a litre? _____

23 A bag contains 24 nuts. Aaron eats $\frac{1}{3}$ of them. Billy eats $\frac{1}{8}$ of them. Safa eats $\frac{1}{2}$ of them.

a) Who eats the most nuts? _____

b) How many more nuts does Aaron eat than Billy? _____

24 Finn mixed some paint. He used $\frac{1}{3}$ l of white paint, $\frac{1}{5}$ l of red paint and $\frac{1}{4}$ l of blue paint. Tick the statement that is true. He used:

more red than blue. ☐   more blue than white. ☐   more white than blue. ☐

UNIT 6 Recognise unit fractions as a division of a quantity

Key point

If the top number (the **numerator**) of a fraction is **1**, it is called a **unit fraction**.

$\frac{1}{3}, \frac{1}{12}, \frac{1}{5}, \frac{1}{9}, \frac{1}{7}$ These are called **unit fractions.**

To find a **unit fraction** of a quantity, divide the **quantity** by the **denominator**.

numerator ⟶ $\frac{1}{10}$ of £50 = £50 ÷ 10 = £5 $\frac{1}{9}$ of 27m = 27m ÷ 9 = 3m
denominator ⟶

Get started

1 Find $\frac{1}{5}$ of 25cm.

_____ cm

2 Find $\frac{1}{10}$ of 70kg.

_____ kg

3 What length is one-fifth of this line?

_____ cm   0 ⊢——┼——┼——┼——⊣ 10cm

4 Find $\frac{1}{2}$ of 74ml.

_____ ml

5 Find one-quarter of 12p.

_____ p

6 Find $\frac{1}{10}$ of 40g.

_____ g

7 Write the missing number.

$\frac{1}{\boxed{}}$ of 12m = 6m

8 Add $\frac{1}{8}$ of 24p to $\frac{1}{4}$ of 24p.

_____ p

Now try these

9 A metre of ribbon costs £4.
What length of ribbon would you get for £1? _____ m

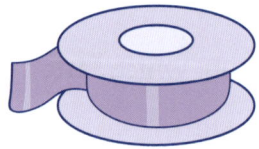

10 How much less than 8cm is $\frac{1}{10}$ of 60cm? _____ cm

11 Find $\frac{1}{3}$ of £9 plus $\frac{1}{3}$ of £6. £_____

12 A right angle is 90°.
How many degrees is half a right angle? _____ °

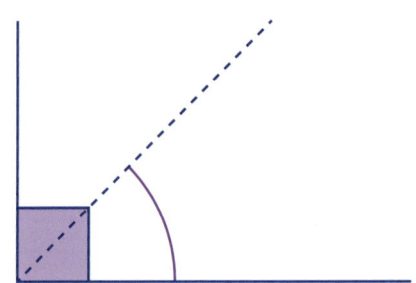

Schofield & Sims Fractions, Decimals and Percentages Fractions 3

13 What is one-third of 27? _____

14 James earns £600. He gives one-tenth of his wages to charity.
How much does he give to charity? £_____

15 Dhruv takes a quarter of the money out of each of these boxes.
How much does he take in total? £_____

16 What is one-fifth of £60? £_____

Challenge

17 One-quarter of a class of 28 children wear glasses.
How many wear glasses? _____

18 The length of a rectangle is 15cm. Its width is one-third of its length.
Find the perimeter of the rectangle. _____ cm

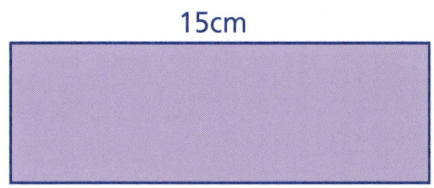

19 Find the difference in kilograms between $\frac{1}{4}$ of 32kg and $\frac{1}{8}$ of 48kg. _____ kg

20 | $\frac{1}{3}$ of £36 $\frac{1}{8}$ of £40 $\frac{1}{10}$ of £110 |

Look at the fractions above. What is the value of the:

a) largest of these amounts? £_____   b) smallest of these amounts? £_____

21 How many minutes is $\frac{1}{6}$ of an hour? _____ min

22 Write the missing number to match this picture.

$\frac{1}{\boxed{}}$ of 18l = 6l

23 Amber divides 60 by 5 to help her answer the question 'What fraction of an hour is 5 minutes?'
Write her answer. _____ hr

24 A 3m length of string is cut into 10 equal pieces. Write the length of each piece:

a) as a fraction of a metre. _____ m

b) in centimetres. _____ cm

15

Check-up test 1

1 Find the value of $\frac{1}{4}$ of these coins. _____ p

2 Tick the container that is about $\frac{3}{4}$ full.

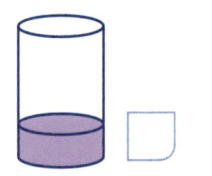   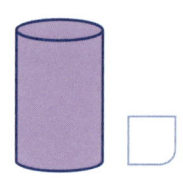

3 A sheet of paper is cut into four equal pieces.
What fraction of the whole sheet is three pieces? _____

4 How many quarters are equal to one-half? _____ quarters

5 True or false? Three-quarters is purple.   True ☐   False ☐

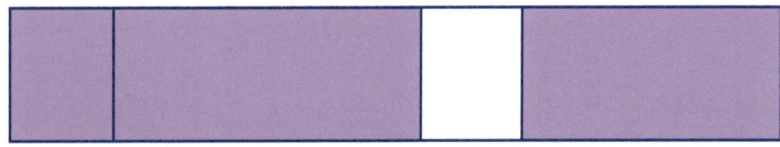

6 Draw a cross on the line to show $2\frac{1}{4}$.

7 How many pence is half of £1? _____ p

8 Write the answer to 1 ÷ 2 as a fraction. _____

9 True or false? $\frac{1}{3}$ of a shape is smaller than $\frac{1}{2}$ of the shape.

True ☐   False ☐

10 One-quarter subtracted from three-quarters is equal to how many halves?
_____ halves

11 An orange is cut into six equal pieces. What fraction of the orange is one piece?

_____

1 mark

12 Tick the circle that has about $\frac{1}{5}$ shaded.

1 mark

13 A 1m plank of wood is cut into eight equal lengths.

What fraction of a metre is each length? _____ m

1 mark

14 True or false? $\frac{1}{3}$ is larger than $\frac{1}{6}$.

True ☐   False ☐

1 mark

15 Two cups are the same size. Cup A is $\frac{1}{5}$ full. Cup B is $\frac{1}{7}$ full.

Which cup contains more? _____

1 mark

16 A bag contains 20 nuts. Jon has $\frac{1}{10}$ of them, Dan has $\frac{1}{2}$ of them and Mia has $\frac{1}{5}$ of them.

a) Who has the most nuts? _____

b) How many more nuts does Mia have than Jon? _____

1 mark

17 Find $\frac{1}{6}$ of 30cm. _____ cm

1 mark

18 What is one-fifth of 20? _____

1 mark

19 How many minutes is $\frac{1}{10}$ of an hour? _____ min

1 mark

20 A 3m length of tinsel is cut into 4 equal pieces. Write the length of each piece:

a) as a fraction of a metre. _____ m

b) in centimetres. _____ cm

1 mark

Total

20 marks

17

UNIT 7 Understand non-unit fractions as areas of shapes

Key point

Unit fractions have the numerator **1**, for example, $\frac{1}{5}$.

$\frac{1}{5}$ is **1 part of a whole** when a whole is split into **5 equal parts**.

When the **numerator** is **not 1**, the fraction means several parts of a whole.
The **numerator** (the top number) shows how many parts are being described.

$\frac{3}{5}$ is **3 parts of a whole** when a whole is split into **5 equal parts**.

Get started

1 What fraction of this shape is purple?

_____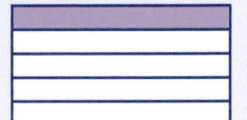

2 Colour three-quarters of this shape.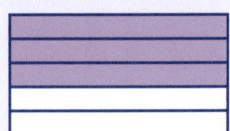

3 True or false? Three-eighths are purple.

True ☐
False ☐

4 Write $\frac{3}{5}$ in words. _____

5 Which shape is $\frac{2}{3}$ purple?

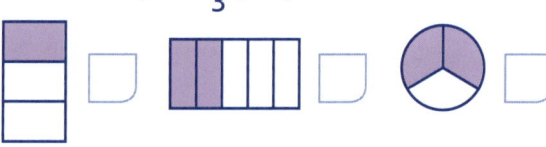

6 Write sixth-sevenths in digits. _____

7 Colour five-ninths of this shape.

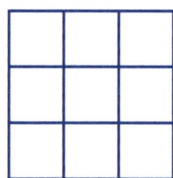

8 Write the numerator of four-fifths.

_____

Now try these

9 A loaf of bread is cut into six equal slices. What fraction of the whole loaf is five slices? _____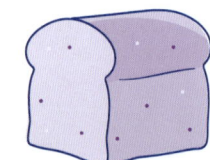

10 Tick the shape that is $\frac{2}{5}$ purple.

11 A block of cheese is cut into eight equal slices. Luke eats five of the slices.

What fraction of the whole cheese does he eat? _____

12 A rope is cut into seven equal lengths.

What fraction of the whole rope is five of the lengths? _____

13 A chocolate bar has 8 chunks. Dev eats $\frac{3}{8}$ of the bar.

What fraction of the bar is left? _____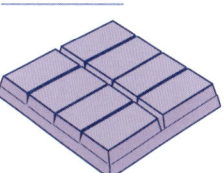

14 Five girls each eat one-sixth of a pie. What fraction is left over? _____

15 What fraction of the cylinder is purple?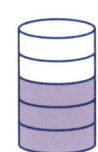

_____

16 True or false? $\frac{1}{4} + \frac{1}{4} + \frac{1}{4} = \frac{3}{4}$ True ☐   False ☐

Challenge

17 A patio is made from nine square tiles, all the same size. One tile is black and the rest are white.

What fraction of the patio is white? _____

18 Cross out the pattern that does not show $\frac{3}{6}$ purple.

19 Colour parts of this shape to show $\frac{7}{9}$.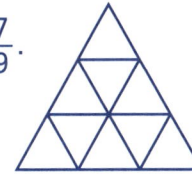

20 To what number will the arrow point after $\frac{3}{8}$ of a turn clockwise?

_____

21 A rug is $\frac{1}{8}$ red, $\frac{3}{8}$ yellow, $\frac{3}{8}$ white and the rest is orange. What fraction is orange? _____

22 How many ninths more than $\frac{1}{9}$ is $\frac{5}{9}$? _____ ninths

23 $\frac{3}{7}$ $\frac{1}{7}$ $\frac{6}{7}$ $\frac{4}{7}$

Look at the fractions above. Which of these fractions is:

a) the largest? _____   b) the smallest? _____

24 The minute hand of this clock turns $\frac{2}{3}$ of a full turn from the top.

What number will it be pointing to? _____

UNIT 8 Recognise tenths and count in tenths

Key point

When something is divided into **10** equal parts each part is called a **tenth**.

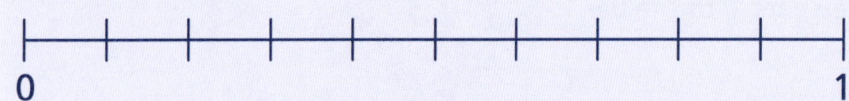

When counting in tenths, every tenth number will be a whole number.

0, $\frac{1}{10}$, $\frac{2}{10}$, $\frac{3}{10}$, $\frac{4}{10}$, $\frac{5}{10}$, $\frac{6}{10}$, $\frac{7}{10}$, $\frac{8}{10}$, $\frac{9}{10}$, **1**, ...

When continuing this sequence remember that $\frac{10}{10}$ and **1** have the same value.

1, $1\frac{1}{10}$, $1\frac{2}{10}$, $1\frac{3}{10}$, $1\frac{4}{10}$ ...   or $\frac{10}{10}$, $\frac{11}{10}$, $\frac{12}{10}$, $\frac{13}{10}$, $\frac{14}{10}$ ...   Both are correct.

Get started

1 How many tenths of the whole are purple?

_____ tenths

2 Write what number the arrow is pointing to.

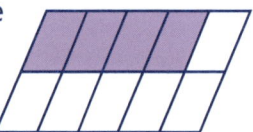

_____

3 What is one-tenth more than $\frac{8}{10}$?

_____

4 What is two-tenths less than one whole?

_____

5 Which number is missing from this sequence?

$\frac{8}{10}$, _____, 1, $1\frac{1}{10}$, $1\frac{2}{10}$

6 How many tenths of a metre make a whole metre?

_____ tenths

7 Write the next number in the sequence.

$3\frac{4}{10}$, $3\frac{5}{10}$, $3\frac{6}{10}$, $3\frac{7}{10}$, _____

8 Colour three more tenths of this circle.

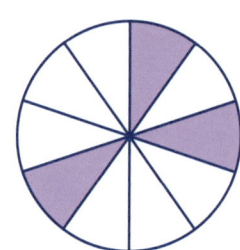

Now try these

9 One-tenth of a kilogram of sand and $\frac{6}{10}$ of a kilogram of cement are put into a bucket. What fraction of a kilogram does the mixture weigh? _____ kg

10 What is $2\frac{9}{10} + \frac{1}{10}$? _____

11. Colour squares so that half of this grid is coloured.
How many tenths are now coloured? _____ tenths

12. How many tenths are in two whole ones? _____ tenths

13. Write the missing number.

    $\frac{12}{10} = 1\frac{\square}{10}$

14. Write the missing number to give the mass shown.

    $8\frac{\square}{10}$ kg

15. How many centimetres in one-tenth of a metre? _____ cm

16. Count back six-tenths from 5. What number do you reach? _____

Challenge

17. What is the difference between one whole and three-tenths? _____

18. Some square carpet tiles have sides that are each $\frac{1}{10}$ of a metre.

    How long is a line of 13 touching tiles, in metres? _____ m

19. Write the missing fractions in this sequence.

    $\frac{15}{10}$, _____, $\frac{13}{10}$, $\frac{12}{10}$, _____, 1

20. True or false? $\frac{5}{10}$ is equal to $\frac{1}{2}$.   True ☐   False ☐

21. If $\frac{1}{10}$ litre of water flows out of a tap every second, how many litres will flow out in 20 seconds?
    _____ l

22. A line is divided into 10 equal parts.
    If nine of the parts measure 9cm in total, what is the length of the whole line? _____ cm

23. Erin ran a race in $10\frac{1}{2}$ seconds. Kelly took four-tenths of a second longer.

    How long did Kelly take? _____ sec

24. How many tenths greater than $3\frac{1}{2}$ is 5? _____ tenths

UNIT 9 Recognise that tenths arise from dividing by 10

Key point

When 1 pie is shared equally between 10 people, each gets one-tenth.

$1 \div 10 = \frac{1}{10}$

When 2 pies are shared equally between 10 people each gets two-tenths, and so on.

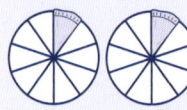
$2 \div 10 = \frac{2}{10}$

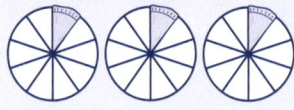
$3 \div 10 = \frac{3}{10}$

Get started

1 $4 \div 10 = \dfrac{\boxed{}}{10}$

2 $7 \div 10 = \dfrac{\boxed{}}{\boxed{}}$

3 What is nine divided by ten, as a fraction? _____

4 $\boxed{} \div 10 = \dfrac{9}{10}$

5 What is 2 melons shared equally between 10, as a fraction? _____

6 What number divided by 10 gives $\dfrac{6}{10}$? _____

7 What is the arrow pointing to? _____

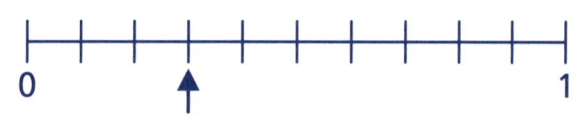

8 Four divided by ten. Write the answer in words. _____

Now try these

9 If 2 cakes are divided equally between 10 people, what fraction of a cake does each get? _____

10 One pot of yoghurt is shared equally into 10 bowls.

What fraction of the pot is in each bowl? _____

11 An 8m rope is cut into 10 equal lengths. What fraction of a metre is each length? _____ m

Schofield & Sims Fractions, Decimals and Percentages Fractions 3

12 A machine makes 10 nails from a piece of metal weighing 9g. What is the weight of each nail as a fraction of a gram? _____ g

13 Dad poured three litres of lemonade equally into 10 cups. How much is there in each cup?

Give your answer as a fraction of a litre. _____ l

14 These five bars of chocolate are split equally between 10 people.

a) How many chunks does each get? _____

b) What fraction of a bar is this? _____

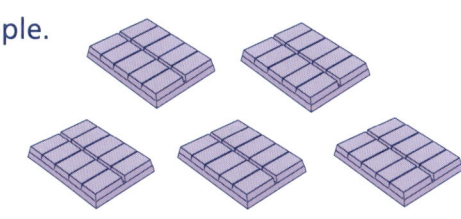

15 Tick which is larger. 3 ÷ 10 ☐ $\frac{2}{10}$ ☐

16 10 sticks are laid touching in a line. Each stick is $\frac{7}{10}$ m long.

What is the length of the line? _____ m

Challenge

17 True or false? 10 lots of $\frac{3}{10}$ is 3 wholes.   True ☐   False ☐

18 A line of 10 squares measures 5m.
How long is each square, as a fraction of a metre? _____ m

19 10 identical boots weigh 4kg in total.
As a fraction of a kilogram, what does one boot weigh? _____ kg

20 As he walks, each of Dominic's steps is $\frac{7}{10}$ m apart.

If he takes 10 steps, how far from the start has he walked? _____ m

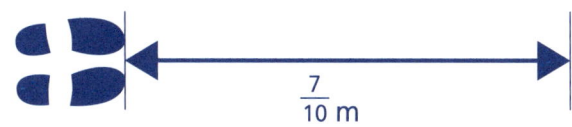

21 Divide five by ten. Circle two correct answers. $\frac{1}{5}$ $\frac{10}{5}$ $\frac{5}{10}$ $\frac{1}{10}$ $\frac{1}{2}$

22 A bag of sugar is 2kg. Each jar holds $\frac{2}{10}$ kg of sugar.

How many jars are needed for all the sugar? _____

23 Luke walks from home to work and back again each day for 5 days. He walks 8km in total. What is the distance from his home to his work, as a fraction of a kilometre? _____ km

24 The digit after a decimal point shows the number of tenths, for example, 0.2 = $\frac{2}{10}$.

Write 0.4 as a fraction. _____

23

UNIT 10 Use fractions as numbers on a number line

Key point

Each whole number on a line can be split into parts and described using fractions.

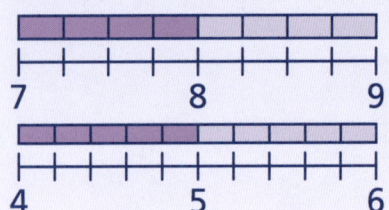

Here each whole is split into **quarters**.

Here each whole is split into **fifths**.

A whole number and a fraction can be used to show points on the line, for example:

$7\frac{1}{4}, 8\frac{3}{4}, 4\frac{3}{5}, 5\frac{4}{5}$ These are called **mixed numbers**.

Get started

1 Write the number shown by the cross on the number line. _____

2 Write the number shown by the arrow on the number line above.

_____

3 How many equal parts is this divided into?

_____

4 What is the missing number?

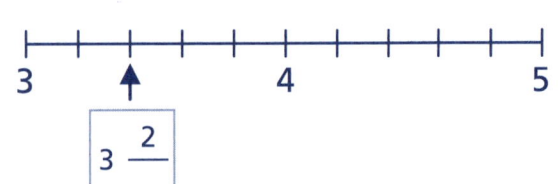

$3\frac{2}{}$

5 What is one-fifth less than 5 wholes?

_____

6 Which number is missing from this sequence?

$0, \frac{1}{5}, \frac{2}{5}, \frac{3}{5}, \frac{4}{5}, 1,$ _____ $, 1\frac{2}{5}$

7 How many equal parts is each whole on this ruler divided into?

_____

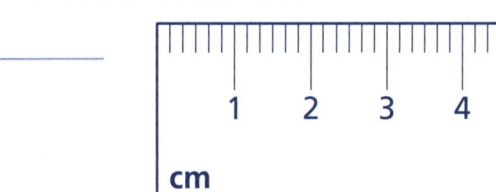

8 What number is the same as five-fifths?

_____

Now try these

9 How many packets are shown? _____

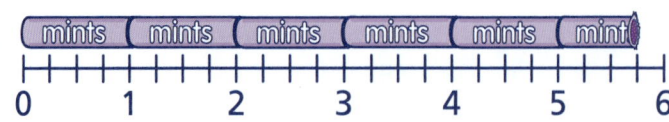

10 What is $\frac{1}{10}$ more than $3\frac{7}{10}$? _____

11 When counting on in sixths, what number comes after 2? _____

12. Write the next two numbers in the sequence. 6, $6\frac{1}{4}$, $6\frac{1}{2}$, $6\frac{3}{4}$, _____, _____

13. How many thirds in two whole ones? _____ thirds

14. Count back three-tenths from two. What number do you reach? _____

15. This ruler shows tenths of a centimetre.
a) Draw a cross to show $\frac{3}{10}$ cm.
b) Draw an arrow to show $1\frac{7}{10}$ cm.

16. How many tenths are there in $2\frac{1}{2}$? _____ tenths

Challenge

17. Count back $\frac{2}{3}$ from 4. What number do you reach? _____

18. What is the difference between $1\frac{1}{5}$ and $1\frac{3}{5}$? _____

19. Count on four-sixths from the arrow on the line. Where do you land? _____

0 1 2 3 4

20. What is $7\frac{7}{8} - \frac{4}{8}$? _____

21. This line is split into twelfths. What is the missing number? $\frac{1}{2} = \frac{\square}{12}$

0   1

22. Toby jumps $4\frac{3}{10}$ m in the long jump and Libby jumps $5\frac{3}{10}$ m.
How much further does Libby jump than Toby? _____ m

23. True or false? $\frac{1}{4} = \frac{2}{8}$
True ☐   False ☐

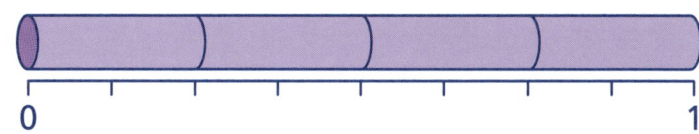

0   1

24. How many fifths greater than 8 is 9? _____ fifths

UNIT 11 Compare fractions with the same denominator

Key point

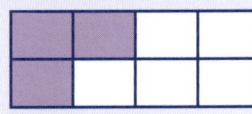 $\frac{3}{8}$ is purple. The shape is split into 8 equal parts (denominator) and 3 of the parts are purple (numerator).

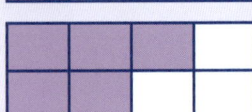 $\frac{5}{8}$ is purple. The shape is split into 8 equal parts (denominator) and 5 of the parts are purple (numerator).

$\frac{3}{8} < \frac{5}{8}$ If the **denominators** are the same, fractions can be compared using just the **numerators**.

Get started

1 True or false? $\frac{5}{8}$ is larger than $\frac{1}{8}$.

True ☐   False ☐

2 Write what fraction of each shape is purple.

a) 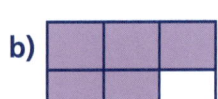 b)

_____   _____

3 Which is more? $\frac{1}{6}$ of an apple or $\frac{5}{6}$ of the same apple? _____

4 Circle the larger fraction. $\frac{3}{5}$ $\frac{2}{5}$

5 Which letter on the number line shows:

a) $\frac{6}{8}$? _____   b) $\frac{4}{8}$? _____

0 A B C D E F G 1

6 True or false? $\frac{5}{10} < \frac{7}{10}$

True ☐   False ☐

7 Use either the < or > sign to show which fraction is larger.

$\frac{5}{4}$ ☐ $\frac{3}{4}$

8 Is $\frac{3}{4}$ of a kilogram more or less than $\frac{1}{4}$ of a kilogram? _____

Now try these

9 Write the fraction of this shape that is:

a) 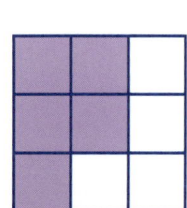 _____   b) ☐ _____

c) Which of these two fractions is larger? _____

10 Tick to show how the fractions in this sequence are ordered: $\frac{1}{5}, \frac{2}{5}, \frac{3}{5}, \frac{4}{5}$

smallest to largest ☐   largest to smallest ☐

11 Mark $\frac{3}{8}$ with a cross and $\frac{7}{8}$ with an arrow on this line.   0  1

12 Circle the fraction that is larger than one-half. $\frac{1}{8}$ $\frac{3}{8}$ $\frac{7}{8}$

13 Three jugs are the same size. Jug A is $\frac{6}{10}$ full. Jug B is $\frac{7}{10}$ full. Jug C is $\frac{10}{10}$ full. Which jug contains most? _____

14 Cross out one of these fractions so that the rest are in order of size. $\frac{3}{10}$ $\frac{4}{10}$ $\frac{6}{10}$ $\frac{2}{10}$ $\frac{9}{10}$

15 Write these fractions from smallest to largest: $\frac{6}{7}$ $\frac{1}{7}$ $\frac{4}{7}$ ☐ ☐ ☐

16 A banana was cut into 9 equal pieces.
Natasha ate $\frac{4}{9}$ of it and Beata ate the rest. Who ate more? _____

Challenge

17 Holly mixed some paint. She used $\frac{3}{8}$l of red paint, $\frac{3}{8}$l of blue paint and $\frac{2}{8}$l of purple paint. Tick the statement that is true. She used:

a) more blue than red. ☐   b) more purple than red. ☐   c) more red than purple. ☐

18 Write these fractions from smallest to largest: $\frac{4}{9}$ $\frac{2}{9}$ $\frac{5}{9}$ $\frac{3}{9}$ ☐ ☐ ☐ ☐

19 Liam says that, because $\frac{4}{8} = \frac{1}{2}$, then $\frac{1}{2} < \frac{5}{8}$.
Is he correct?   Yes ☐   No ☐

20 Each whole is split into 5 equal parts on a number line.
Crosses are marked at three points: $\frac{4}{5}$, $1\frac{1}{5}$ and $\frac{2}{5}$.
Write these numbers from smallest to largest. _____ _____ _____

21 A set contains 12 cards. Connor has $\frac{5}{12}$ of them, Marta has $\frac{4}{12}$ of them and Jamie has the rest of them.

a) Who has the most cards? _____   b) How many cards has Jamie? _____

22 True or false? The largest fraction here plus the smallest fraction is equal to one whole.
$\frac{3}{6}$ $\frac{5}{6}$ $\frac{2}{6}$ $\frac{1}{6}$ $\frac{4}{6}$ True ☐   False ☐

23 Jessica says that $\frac{4}{5}$ of an amount of money is always larger than $\frac{1}{5}$ of a different amount of money. Is she correct?   Yes ☐   No ☐

24 Find $\frac{1}{5}$ of 30p and $\frac{4}{5}$ of 5p.

Write which is larger. _____

UNIT 12 Recognise fractions of a set of objects

Key point

To find fractions of sets of objects, arrange them into **equal groups**.

To find **one-fifth** of these 10 faces, group them into **5 groups**.

$\frac{1}{5}$ (1 group) of the **10** faces is **2** faces.

$\frac{3}{5}$ (3 groups) of the **10** faces is **6** faces.

Get started

1 True or false? The 3 purple faces are $\frac{1}{4}$ of all the faces.

True ☐

False ☐

2 What fraction of the cubes are purple?

_____

3 Colour some more cubes above so that now $\frac{3}{5}$ of the cubes are coloured.

4 What fraction of these cats have:

a) collars? _____

b) no collars? _____

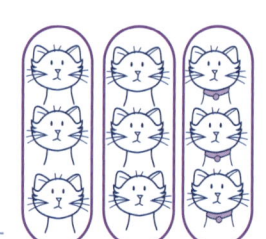

5 Draw more loops on this grid to show 5 equal groups.

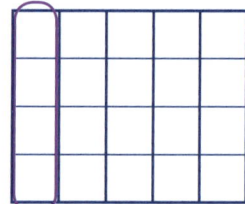

6 Now colour $\frac{1}{5}$ of the squares in the grid above.

7 Draw more loops on this grid to show quarters.

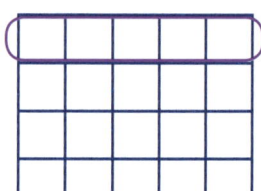

8 Now colour $\frac{3}{4}$ of the squares in the grid above.

Now try these

9 Draw loops around the sweets to split them equally into three groups.

10 How many is one-third of the 6 sweets? _____

11 12 grapes are arranged into 6 equal groups. How many is $\frac{1}{6}$ of the 12 grapes? _____

12 Tick which tile pattern shows $\frac{1}{6}$ purple.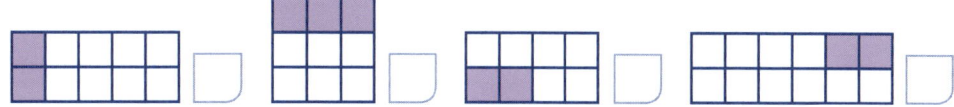

13 How many equal groups are some objects sorted into to show eighths? _____

14 There are 16 beads on this necklace.

Colour $\frac{1}{8}$ of the beads.

Draw crosses on $\frac{3}{8}$ of the beads.

15 What fraction of these 8 balls are white?
_____

16 What fraction of these 24 balls are white?

_____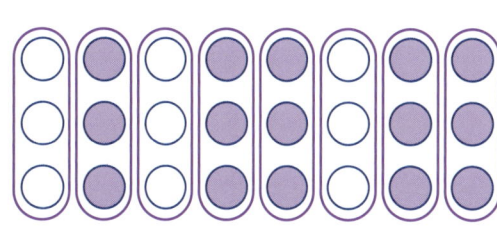

Challenge

17 A book has 25 pages. Lauren has read 5 pages. What fraction of the book has she:

a) read? _____ b) not read? _____

18 Colour $\frac{5}{6}$ of the 24 squares in this grid.

19 How many is $\frac{5}{6}$ of 24? _____

20 What is one-third of 30 sheep? _____

21 A bag contains 2 red apples, 6 yellow apples and 8 green apples. What fraction of the apples are:

a) red? _____ b) green? _____

22 Write the fraction of stars that are white.

a) 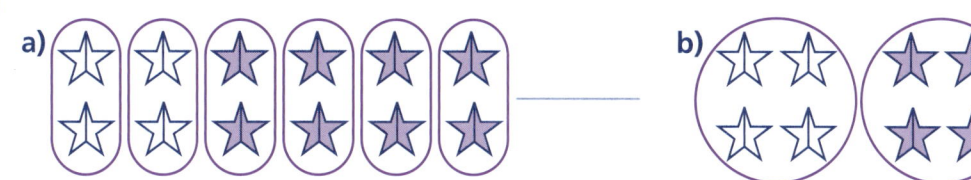 _____ b)  _____

23 Zain has £1 in 1p coins. He sorts the coins into 10 equal piles. What is the value of the coins in:

a) one pile? _____ p b) three piles? _____ p

24 What is $\frac{3}{10}$ of £1? _____ p

Check-up test 2

1 What fraction of the shape is purple? _____

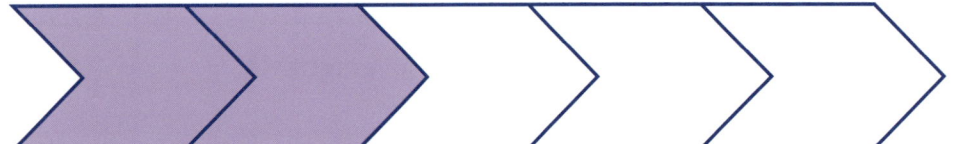

2 Write $\frac{3}{8}$ in words. _____

3 Six boys each take one-seventh of a pitta bread.

What fraction is left over? _____

4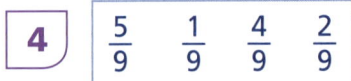

Look at the fractions above. Which is:

a) the largest? _____   b) the smallest? _____

5 What is six-tenths less than one whole? _____

6 Colour six more tenths of this circle.

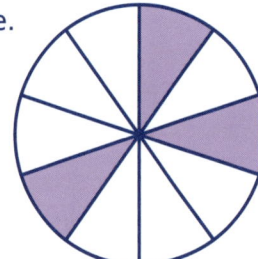

7 What is $2\frac{3}{10} + \frac{1}{10}$? _____

8 True or false? $\frac{5}{10}$ is equal to $\frac{1}{2}$.   True ☐   False ☐

9 What is seven divided by ten, as a fraction? _____

10 A bag of rice is 3kg. Each jar holds $\frac{3}{10}$ kg of rice.

How many jars are needed for all the rice? _____

1 mark (×10)

11 Write the number shown by the arrow. _____

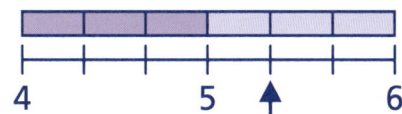

12 What is $\frac{1}{10}$ more than $2\frac{3}{10}$? _____

13 What is the difference between $1\frac{4}{5}$ and $1\frac{3}{5}$? _____

14 Circle the larger fraction. $\frac{4}{7}$ $\frac{6}{7}$

15 Circle the fraction that is larger than one-half. $\frac{2}{6}$ $\frac{1}{6}$ $\frac{4}{6}$

16 Adam says that $\frac{3}{4}$ of an amount of money is always larger than $\frac{1}{4}$ of a different amount of money. Is he correct?

Yes ☐   No ☐

17 What fraction of the cubes are purple? _____

18 How many is one-fifth of 10 ice creams? _____

19 What fraction of these 8 frogs are jumping? _____

20 Colour $\frac{3}{8}$ of the 24 squares in this grid.

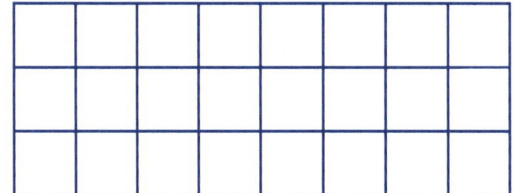

1 mark (×10)

Total

20 marks

31

UNIT 13 Use non-unit fractions in a variety of representations

Key point

Fractions involve a **whole** being split into **equal parts**. Here different wholes are all split into **5** equal parts. Each part is **one-fifth**.

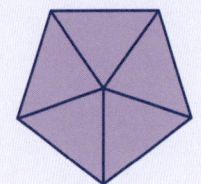

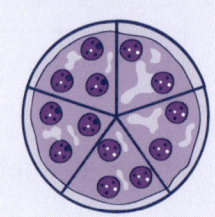
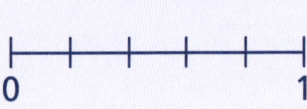
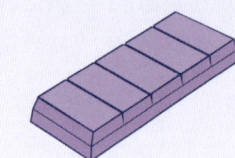

Get started

1 What fraction of these flags are white?

_____

2 Tick the shape that is $\frac{4}{6}$ purple.

3 Circle the fraction made when three wholes are divided by 10. $\frac{10}{3}$ $\frac{1}{3}$ $\frac{3}{10}$

4 Colour five-twelfths of this shape.

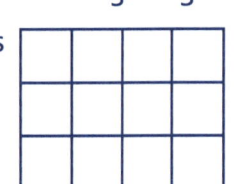

5 What is one-fifth of 15? _____

6 Draw a cross at $\frac{3}{4}$ on this line.

7 What fraction of the cubes are purple?

_____

8 One whole pound is split into tenths.

How much is one-tenth? _____ p

Now try these

9 A cake is cut into six equal slices. What fraction of the whole cake is five slices? _____

10 If A stands for $\frac{1}{5}$, what does B stand for? _____

```
├────┼──A──B──┼────┼────┤
0                        1
```

11 Draw a cross on the line above to show four-fifths.

12 True or false? $\frac{1}{5} + \frac{1}{5} + \frac{1}{5} = \frac{3}{5}$ True ☐   False ☐

Schofield & Sims **Fractions, Decimals and Percentages** Fractions 3

13 Which letter on the number line shows $\frac{5}{8}$? _____   0 A B C D E F G 1

14 What fraction does C represent on the number line above? _____

15 There are 4 yellow tennis balls and 3 green ones.

What fraction of the balls are green? _____

16 A piece of string is cut into eight equal lengths.
What fraction of the whole piece of string are three of the lengths together? _____

Challenge

17 What fraction of a week is: **a)** one day? _____   **b)** two days? _____

18 A group of 10 children get into pairs.
What fraction of the group is:

a) one pair? _____

b) four pairs? _____

19 Jonah eats $\frac{3}{10}$ of a chocolate bar. What fraction is left? _____

20 What fraction do you get if you divide eight by ten?

Write the answer in words. _____

21 Colour $\frac{5}{6}$ of the 18 squares in this grid.

22 How many times as long as $\frac{1}{10}$ of a kilometre is $\frac{3}{10}$ of a kilometre? _____

23 | $\frac{3}{7}$ | $\frac{1}{7}$ | $\frac{6}{7}$ | $\frac{4}{7}$ |

Look at the fractions above. Which of these fractions is:

a) the largest? _____   **b)** the smallest? _____

24 One-third of Macy's money is 10p.

a) How much is $\frac{2}{3}$ of her money? _____ p

b) How much is the whole amount of her money? _____ p

33

UNIT 14 Recognise fractions showing the same amount

Key point

Parts of these two shapes are purple and white.

The first shape is $\frac{1}{4}$ purple and $\frac{3}{4}$ white.

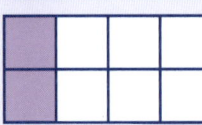
The second shape is $\frac{2}{8}$ purple and $\frac{6}{8}$ white.

The same amount of each shape is purple. $\frac{1}{4}$ is the same amount as $\frac{2}{8}$.

The same amount of each shape is white. $\frac{3}{4}$ is the same amount as $\frac{6}{8}$.

Get started

1 Do these two shapes show the same amount purple?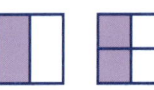

Yes ☐ No ☐

2 How many quarters are the same as one-half? _____ quarters

3 Do these two shapes have the same amount purple?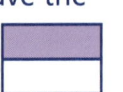

Yes ☐ No ☐

4 One-half is the same as how many sixths? _____ sixths

5 What number is missing?

$\frac{1}{2}$ is the same amount as $\frac{\square}{6}$.

6 Do these two shapes show the same amount purple?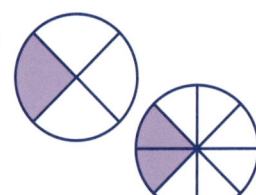

Yes ☐ No ☐

7 $\frac{1}{4}$ is the same amount as $\frac{\square}{8}$.

8 How many eighths are the same amount as one-half? _____ eighths

Now try these

9 Three-quarters is how many eighths? _____ eighths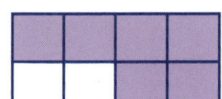

10 How many tenths is the same as one-half?

$\frac{1}{2} = \frac{\square}{10}$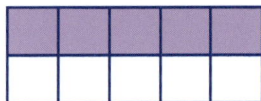

11 This cylinder is $\frac{3}{6}$ purple. Write another fraction to show what fraction of the cylinder is purple. _____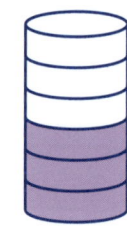

Schofield & Sims Fractions, Decimals and Percentages Fractions 3

12 Look at the shapes and write the missing numbers.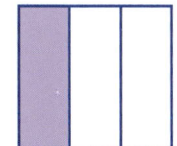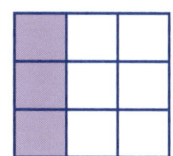

$\frac{1}{\boxed{}}$ is the same amount as $\frac{3}{\boxed{}}$.

13 A cereal bar has 8 chunks. Kim eats one-quarter of the whole bar.

How many chunks does she eat? _____

14 A tart is cut into six equal slices. Aswin's family eat half of the tart.

How many slices do they eat? _____

15 David's birthday cake is cut into equal slices.
He eats $\frac{2}{8}$ of the cake. Is this more, less or the same as $\frac{1}{4}$ of the cake? _____

16 For each diagram, write the fraction of the shape that is purple.

a)    b) 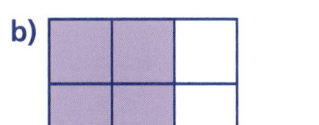   c)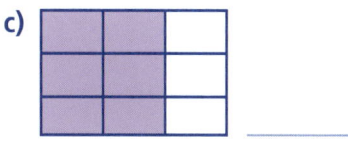

Challenge

17 Eight-twelfths is the same
amount as how many thirds? _____ thirds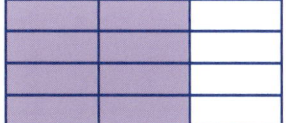

18 A number line shows tenths.
How many tenths are the same as one-half? _____ tenths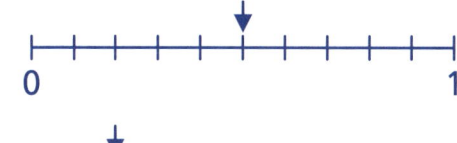

19 A number line is split into fifths.
How many tenths are the same as one-fifth? _____ tenths

20 What is the missing number? $\frac{4}{5}$ is the same as $\frac{\boxed{}}{10}$.

21 Colour one-quarter of this rectangle.

22 How many twelfths have you coloured above? _____ twelfths

23 What fraction of the rectangle above is not coloured? $\frac{\boxed{}}{12} = \frac{\boxed{}}{4}$

24 A wall is covered in tiles. $\frac{3}{12}$ of the tiles are white. $\frac{1}{4}$ of the tiles are pink.
Are there the same number of white tiles as pink tiles? Yes ☐ No ☐

35

UNIT 15 Find equivalent fractions using a fraction wall

Key point

Fractions are called **equivalent** when they stand for the **same** amount.

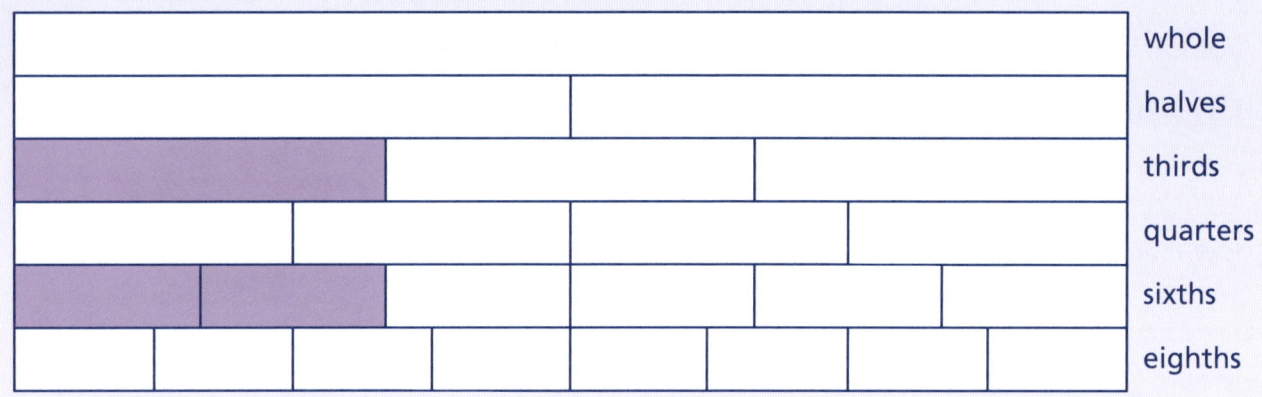

	whole
	halves
	thirds
	quarters
	sixths
	eighths

The purple bars show that $\frac{1}{3}$ and $\frac{2}{6}$ are **equivalent**.

Get started

1 Use the fraction wall to help you find how many quarters are equivalent to one-half. _____ quarters

2 One-half is equivalent to how many sixths? _____ sixths

3 One-quarter is equivalent to how many eighths? _____ eighths

4 One-third is equivalent to how many sixths? _____ sixths

5 The fraction $\frac{1}{2}$ is equivalent to how many eighths?
_____ eighths

6 $\frac{1}{4}$ is equivalent to $\frac{\square}{8}$.

7 $\frac{2}{3}$ is equivalent to $\frac{\square}{6}$.

8 How many quarters are equivalent to one whole?
_____ quarters

Now try these

9 One-quarter of this shape is purple.
How many eighths is this? _____ eighths

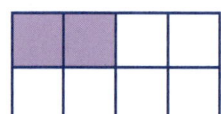

10 Colour one-half of these rectangles.

Now write the missing number. $\frac{1}{2} = \frac{\square}{6}$

11 How many tenths are equivalent to three-fifths? $\frac{3}{5} = \frac{\square}{10}$

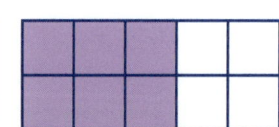

Schofield & Sims Fractions, Decimals and Percentages Fractions 3

12 Six of these 15 buttons are white. The buttons are grouped into fifths.

How many fifths are white? $\frac{6}{15} = \frac{\Box}{5}$

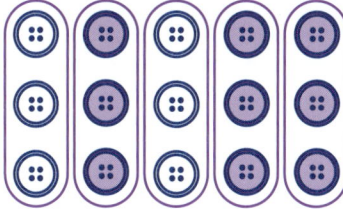

13 Nine of the 15 buttons are purple.

How many fifths are purple? $\frac{9}{15} = \frac{\Box}{5}$

14 Write a fraction with the denominator 9 that is equivalent to $\frac{1}{3}$.

$\frac{1}{3} = \frac{\Box}{\Box}$

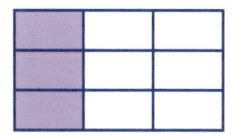

15 There are 16 beads on this necklace. Colour 8 of the beads. Write two equivalent fractions to show what fraction of the beads are coloured in. _____ _____

16 Now draw crosses on 4 of the beads. Write two equivalent fractions to show what fraction of the beads have crosses. _____ _____

Challenge

17 One-fifth of the grid is purple. $\frac{1}{5} = \frac{\Box}{10}$

18 Four-fifths of the grid is white. $\frac{4}{5} = \frac{\Box}{10}$

19 Some friends share a birthday cake. Olivia has $\frac{2}{8}$ of it. Brooke has $\frac{1}{4}$ of it.

Do they have the same amount?   Yes ☐   No ☐

20 What is the missing numerator? $\frac{3}{4} = \frac{\Box}{8}$

21 For each diagram, write the fraction of bow ties that are white.

a)   b)   c)

$\frac{4}{\Box} = \frac{2}{\Box} = \frac{1}{\Box}$

22 What fraction of each set of bow ties above are purple?   a) _____   b) _____   c) _____

23 Complete this pattern. $\frac{1}{2} = \frac{\Box}{4} = \frac{\Box}{8}$

24 Two of these fractions are equivalent to one-half. Circle them. $\frac{2}{3}$ $\frac{5}{10}$ $\frac{3}{8}$ $\frac{4}{4}$ $\frac{4}{6}$ $\frac{6}{12}$

UNIT 16 Add fractions with the same denominator

Key point

When adding fractions ask: 'Are the denominators the same?'

If so, **add the numerators only**. Use the **same denominator**.

numerator → $\dfrac{3}{10} + \dfrac{6}{10} = \dfrac{9}{10}$
denominator →

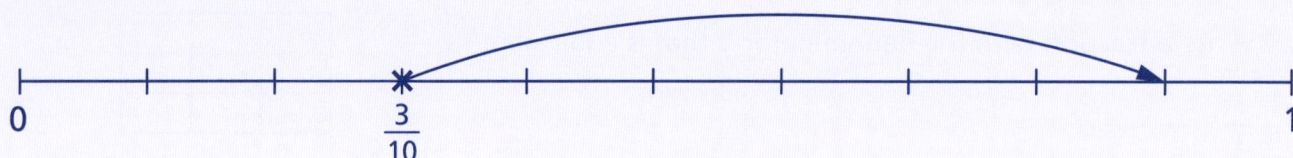

Get started

1) $\dfrac{2}{7} + \dfrac{3}{7} = \dfrac{\boxed{}}{7}$

2) $\dfrac{1}{10} + \dfrac{6}{10} = \boxed{}$

3) $\dfrac{1}{8}$ plus $\dfrac{4}{8}$ = _____

4) Add $\dfrac{1}{3}$ and $\dfrac{1}{3}$. _____

5) $\dfrac{\boxed{}}{9} + \dfrac{3}{9} = \dfrac{8}{9}$

6) Double $\dfrac{2}{5}$. _____

7) $\dfrac{1}{8} + \dfrac{1}{8} + \dfrac{3}{8} = \boxed{}$

8) $\dfrac{4}{12} + \boxed{} = \dfrac{11}{12}$

Now try these

9) Write the fraction of this shape that is:

a) ▨ _____   b) ▧ _____   c) ▨ or ▧ _____

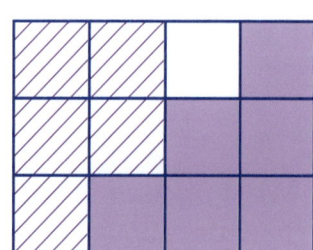

10) Count on $\dfrac{4}{6}$ from $\dfrac{1}{6}$. _____

11) What is added to $\dfrac{1}{11}$ to get $\dfrac{9}{11}$? _____

38

12 Increase five-sevenths by one-seventh. _____

13 What is $\frac{2}{9}$ more than $\frac{5}{9}$? _____

14 Find the sum of four-ninths and three-ninths. _____

15 Find the total of $\frac{2}{6}$ and $\frac{3}{6}$. _____

16 Give the sum of $\frac{5}{12}$ and $\frac{7}{12}$ as a whole number. _____

Challenge

17 $\frac{1}{10}$m is added to $\frac{6}{10}$m. What fraction of a metre is still required to make 1 metre? _____ m

18 Find the values of *a* and *b*.
$\frac{1}{10} + \frac{4}{10} = \frac{a}{10} = \frac{1}{b}$ a = _____   b = _____

19 Amina mixes one-quarter of a kilogram of sugar with two-quarters of a kilogram of flour.

How many grams is the total mixture? _____ g

20 How many quarters are equivalent to the sum of $\frac{1}{8}$, $\frac{3}{8}$ and $\frac{2}{8}$? _____ quarters

21 A line is 0.4cm. What is the length of another line that is three-tenths of a centimetre longer? Give your answer as a fraction. _____ cm

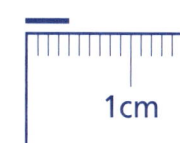

1cm

22 Ollie spent $\frac{1}{6}$ of an hour watching a cartoon and $\frac{2}{6}$ of an hour watching a quiz show.

a) For what fraction of an hour did he watch altogether? _____ hr

b) How many minutes is this? _____ min

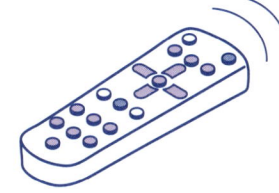

23 Write the answer to $\frac{1}{12} + \frac{5}{12}$ as a fraction with the numerator 1. _____

24 Which two different fractions with the denominator 10 have a total that is equivalent to two-fifths?

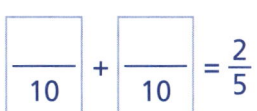

UNIT 17 Subtract fractions with the same denominator

Key point

When subtracting fractions ask: '*Are the denominators the same?*'

If so, **subtract the numerators only**. Use the **same denominator**.

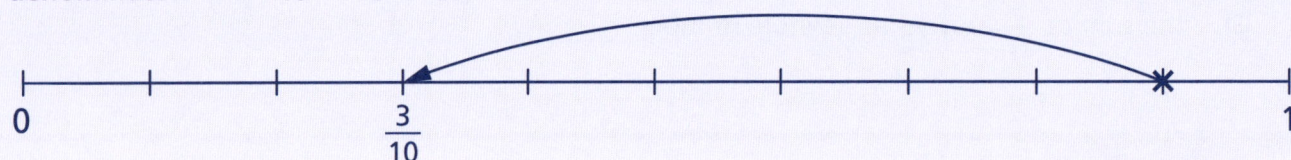

Get started

1. $\dfrac{6}{7} - \dfrac{3}{7} = \dfrac{\Box}{7}$

2. $\dfrac{8}{10} - \dfrac{1}{10} = \dfrac{\Box}{\Box}$

3. $\dfrac{7}{8}$ minus $\dfrac{4}{8} = \dfrac{\Box}{\Box}$

4. Subtract $\dfrac{1}{3}$ from $\dfrac{2}{3}$. _____

5. $\dfrac{\Box}{9} - \dfrac{3}{9} = \dfrac{2}{9}$

6. $\dfrac{8}{8} - \dfrac{1}{8} = \dfrac{\Box}{\Box}$

7. Take $\dfrac{2}{5}$ from one whole. _____

8. $\dfrac{9}{12} - \dfrac{\Box}{\Box} = \dfrac{2}{12}$

Now try these

9. Decrease five-sevenths by one-seventh. _____

10. Count back $\dfrac{4}{6}$ from $\dfrac{5}{6}$. _____

11. What is subtracted from $\dfrac{9}{11}$ to get $\dfrac{1}{11}$? _____

12. What is $\dfrac{5}{5}$ minus $\dfrac{2}{5}$?

_____

Schofield & Sims Fractions, Decimals and Percentages Fractions 3

13 What is $\frac{2}{9}$ less than $\frac{7}{9}$? _____

14 Find the difference between four-ninths and three-ninths. _____

15 A bag of flour weighs $\frac{8}{10}$ kg. Kyle uses $\frac{3}{10}$ kg of the flour to make a cake.

  a) What fraction of a kilogram is left? _____ kg

  b) How many grams is this? _____ g

16 Zoë walks $\frac{3}{8}$ of the way to school. What fraction is left to walk? _____

Challenge

17 Maria spent $\frac{7}{12}$ of an hour listening to music. For $\frac{1}{12}$ of an hour she listened to hip hop and for the rest of the time she listened to jazz.

  a) For what fraction of an hour did she listen to jazz? _____ hr

  b) How many minutes is this? _____ min

18 Find the values of a and b.

  $\frac{9}{10} - \frac{7}{10} = \frac{a}{10} = \frac{1}{b}$ $a =$ _____ $b =$ _____

19 Write the answer to $\frac{11}{12} - \frac{5}{12}$ as a fraction with the numerator 1. _____

20 A lorry driver has to travel from one city to another. He drives $\frac{3}{9}$ of the distance before lunch and finishes his journey after lunch.

  a) What fraction of the way does he drive after lunch? _____

  b) How many thirds of the distance is this? _____ thirds

21 $\frac{3}{6}$ $\frac{5}{6}$ $\frac{2}{6}$ $\frac{1}{6}$ $\frac{4}{6}$

  What is the largest fraction minus the smallest fraction? _____

22 A line is 0.4 cm. What is the length of another line that is three-tenths of a centimetre shorter? Give your answer as a fraction. _____ cm

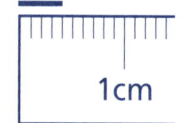

1cm

23 Only $\frac{7}{12}$ of the seats for a football match were sold.

Some of the seats were sold to women, $\frac{4}{12}$ were sold to men and $\frac{2}{12}$ to children.

What fraction of the seats were sold to women? _____

24 $1 - \frac{3}{7} + \frac{2}{7} - \frac{4}{7} = \boxed{}$

41

UNIT 18 Solve problems with measures

Key point

Fractions can be used to show parts of a whole **unit of measurement** such as a kilogram, a metre, a litre or a centimetre.

For example: $\frac{1}{4}$ kg or $\frac{3}{10}$ cm

Whole numbers and fractions can be used together (as **mixed numbers**) to show measurements **larger than one unit**.

For example: $3\frac{1}{2}$ kg or $5\frac{7}{10}$ cm

When using tenths, a **decimal** can be used.

For example: $5\frac{7}{10}$ cm = 5.7cm

Get started

1. Write two and three-quarter centimetres in digits. _____ cm

2. Write this measurement in words: $6\frac{1}{2}$ kg.
   _____

3. How many quarters of a kilogram are in 2 kilograms?
   _____ quarters

4. Write two-fifths of a metre in digits.
   _____ m 0 ├─┼─┼─┼─┼─┤ 1

5. What length is $\frac{3}{8}$ m more than 3m?
   _____ m

6. What capacity is $\frac{1}{4}$ litre more than 4 litres? _____ l

7. True or false? $\frac{3}{6}$ litre = $\frac{1}{2}$ litre
   True ☐   False ☐

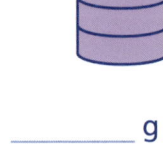

8. How many grams in $\frac{1}{2}$ kg? _____ g

Now try these

9. This line is 0.7cm.
   Write its length as a fraction of a centimetre. _____ cm

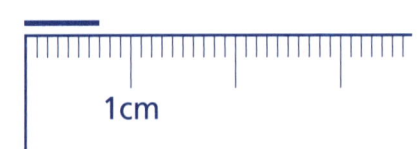
1cm

10. How many tenths of a centimetre make half a centimetre? _____ tenths

11. A metre is divided into 10 equal parts. How many centimetres is the same as $\frac{3}{10}$ m? _____ cm

Schofield & Sims Fractions, Decimals and Percentages Fractions 3

12 How many minutes is:

a) $\frac{1}{4}$ hour? _____ min   b) $\frac{1}{2}$ hour? _____ min   c) $1\frac{1}{2}$ hours? _____ min

13 What length of time is $\frac{1}{4}$ hour plus $1\frac{1}{4}$ hours? _____ hr

14 A 1m plank of wood is sawn into six equal lengths.

What fraction of a metre is each length? _____ m

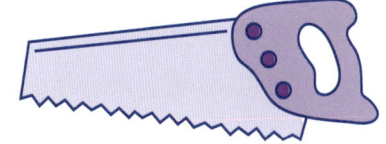

15 A tap pours $\frac{1}{10}$ litre of water every second.

How many litres will it pour in 60 seconds? _____ l

16 Write five-tenths of a centimetre as a decimal. _____ cm

Challenge

17 Circle the heaviest mass. $4\frac{5}{8}$ kg $3\frac{1}{3}$ kg $4\frac{7}{8}$ kg

18 Find the difference in grams between $\frac{1}{4}$ of 32g and $\frac{1}{8}$ of 48g. _____ g

19 As he walks, each of Omar's steps is $\frac{1}{4}$ m apart.

If he takes 9 steps, how far from the start has he walked? _____ m

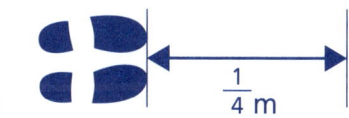

20 What is one-eighth of a litre less than 2 litres? _____ l

21 The length of a rectangle is 9cm. Its width is $\frac{1}{3}$ of its length.

Find the perimeter of the rectangle. _____ cm

22 Some square cards have sides that are each $\frac{1}{10}$ of a metre.

How long is a line of 19 touching cards, in metres? _____ m

23 Lily ran a race in $10\frac{1}{2}$ seconds.

Keira took two-tenths of a second longer.

How long did Keira take? _____ sec

24 How many centimetres less than 1 metre is nine-tenths of a metre? _____ cm

43

Check-up test 3

1 Colour seven-twelfths of this shape.

2 What is one-sixth of 18? _____

3 There are 5 purple socks and 4 white socks.

What fraction of the socks are white? _____

4 $\frac{1}{5}$ of Theo's money is 20p.

a) How much is $\frac{2}{5}$ of his money? _____ p

b) How much is the whole amount of his money? £ _____

5 $\frac{1}{3}$ is the same amount as $\boxed{}/6$.

6 A number line shows tenths. How many tenths is the same as one-fifth?

_____ tenths

7 One-half is equivalent to how many eighths? _____ eighths

8 Some friends share an orange. Emily has $\frac{3}{12}$. Max has $\frac{1}{3}$ of it.

Do they have the same amount?   Yes ☐   No ☐

9 One-quarter is purple. How many twelfths is this?

_____ twelfths

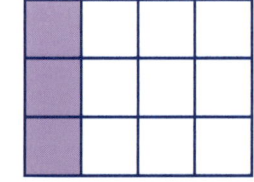

10 $\frac{1}{10} + \frac{8}{10} = \boxed{/}$

11 For each diagram, write the fraction of toy cars that are purple.

a) b) c)

$$\frac{8}{\Box} = \frac{4}{\Box} = \frac{2}{\Box}$$

1 mark

12 Find the difference between two-sevenths and six-sevenths. _____

1 mark

13 $\frac{1}{10}$ m is added to $\frac{2}{10}$ m.

What fraction of a metre is still required to make 1 metre? _____ m

1 mark

14 Subtract $\frac{1}{5}$ from $\frac{3}{5}$. _____

1 mark

15 Nadia eats $\frac{2}{9}$ of an apple. What fraction is left? _____

1 mark

16 A box of washing powder weighs $\frac{7}{10}$ kg.
Thomas uses $\frac{2}{10}$ kg to do the laundry.

a) What fraction of a kilogram is left? _____ kg

b) How many grams is this? _____ g

1 mark

17 Write this measurement in words: $5\frac{1}{4}$ kg _____

1 mark

18 This line is 0.4 cm. Write its length as a fraction of a centimetre.

_____ cm

1cm

1 mark

19 A hosepipe pours $\frac{1}{5}$ litre of water every second.

How many litres will it pour in 60 seconds? _____ l

1 mark

20 How many centimetres less than 1 metre is seven-tenths of a metre? _____ cm

1 mark

Total

20 marks

Final test

Section 1

1 What fraction of the whole shape is purple? _____

1 mark

2 Write the next two numbers in the sequence.

$5\frac{4}{10}, 5\frac{5}{10}, 5\frac{6}{10}, 5\frac{7}{10}, 5\frac{8}{10},$ _____ , _____

1 mark

3 Three pizzas are equally shared between 10 people.

What fraction of a pizza does each get? _____

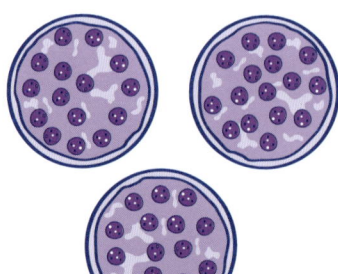

1 mark

4 7kg ÷ 10 = ☐——☐ kg

1 mark

Section 2

5 What fraction of these pencil sharpeners are white? _____

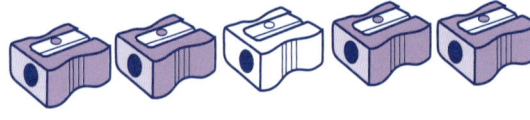

1 mark

6 What fraction of the cubes are purple? _____

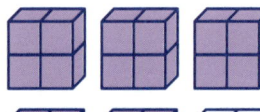

1 mark

7 What is one-quarter of 8 peanuts? _____

1 mark

8 Colour $\frac{2}{5}$ of the 20 squares in this grid.

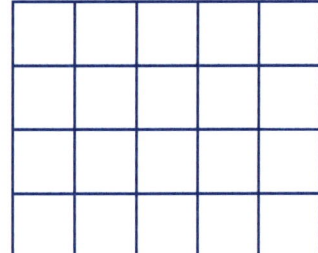

1 mark

46

Schofield & Sims Fractions, Decimals and Percentages Fractions 3

Section 3

9 This ruler shows tenths of a centimetre. Mark $\frac{7}{10}$ cm with a cross and $1\frac{1}{10}$ cm with an arrow on this ruler.

 1 mark

10 What number is the arrow showing?

_____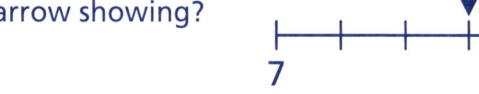

 1 mark

11 What fraction is the answer to 1 ÷ 5? _____

 1 mark

12 Mark the number $2\frac{2}{3}$ on this line with a cross.

 1 mark

Section 4

13 One-quarter is how many eighths?

_____ eighths

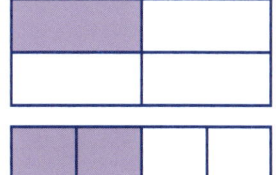

 1 mark

14 $\boxed{\dfrac{2}{}}$ is equivalent to $\boxed{\dfrac{6}{}}$.

 1 mark

15 Circle the fractions that are equivalent to one-half.

$\frac{2}{3}$ $\frac{5}{10}$ $\frac{3}{6}$ $\frac{4}{4}$ $\frac{4}{6}$ $\frac{6}{12}$

 1 mark

16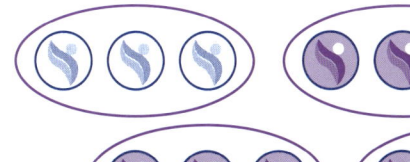

please turn over

47

Final test

Section 5

17 What is two-sevenths more than three-sevenths? _____

1 mark

18 Decrease two-thirds by one-third. _____

1 mark

19 $\dfrac{1}{8} + \dfrac{1}{8} + \dfrac{5}{8} = \boxed{}$

1 mark

20 $\dfrac{11}{12} - \dfrac{4}{12} = \boxed{}$

1 mark

Section 6

21 Is one-sixth of a kilogram more or less than one-quarter of a kilogram? _____

1 mark

22 Tick to show how the fractions in this sequence are ordered:

$\dfrac{1}{6} \quad \dfrac{1}{5} \quad \dfrac{1}{4} \quad \dfrac{1}{3} \quad \dfrac{1}{2}$

smallest to largest ☐

largest to smallest ☐

1 mark

23 Use either the < or > sign to show which is larger.

$\dfrac{5}{7} \;\boxed{}\; \dfrac{3}{7}$

1 mark

24 Write these fractions from smallest to largest:

$\dfrac{4}{10} \quad \dfrac{2}{10} \quad \dfrac{5}{10} \quad \dfrac{3}{10}$ _____ _____ _____ _____

1 mark

48

Section 7

25 10 bricks weigh 9kg in total. What does one brick weigh?

Give your answer as a fraction of a kilogram. _____ kg

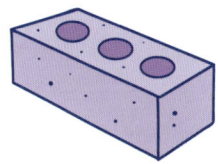

1 mark

26 A bag contains 2 red apples, 6 yellow apples and some green apples. There are 16 apples in the bag.

What fraction of the apples are green? _____

1 mark

27 A tart was cut into 9 equal slices.

Leo ate $\frac{4}{9}$ of it and James ate the rest.

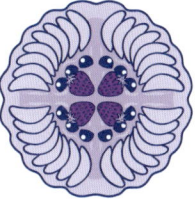

a) Who ate more? _____

b) How much more did he eat as a fraction of the whole pie? _____

1 mark

28 Jo swam a race in $8\frac{1}{2}$ seconds.

Molly took three-tenths of a second longer.

How long did Molly take? _____ sec

1 mark

Total

28 marks

End of test

How did I find it?

Unit		Difficult	Getting there	Easy
1	I can recognise quarters as fractions of shapes.			
2	I can recognise halves and quarters of sets.			
3	I can count up and down in halves and quarters.			
4	I can work with fractions with the numerator 1.			
5	I can compare fractions with the numerator 1.			
6	I can find unit fractions of quantities by dividing.			
	Check-up test 1			
7	I can recognise non-unit fractions as areas of shapes.			
8	I can recognise tenths and count in tenths.			
9	I can recognise that tenths arise from dividing by 10.			
10	I can use fractions as numbers on a number line.			
11	I can compare fractions with the same denominator.			
12	I can find fractions of sets of objects.			
	Check-up test 2			
13	I can use fractions in a range of representations.			
14	I can recognise fractions showing the same amount.			
15	I can identify equivalent fractions using diagrams.			
16	I can add fractions with the same denominator.			
17	I can subtract fractions with the same denominator.			
18	I can solve problems with measures.			
	Check-up test 3			
	Final test	Difficult	Getting there	Easy

Glossary

decimal	A number written with one or more digits after a decimal point is called a decimal. The digit to the right of the decimal point is the tenths digit and shows how many tenths.
decimal point	The dot that lies between the ones digit and the tenths digit of a decimal is called a decimal point. It separates the whole from the parts of a whole.
denominator	The number on the bottom of a fraction is called the denominator. It shows how many equal parts the whole is split into.
equivalent	When two things are equal in value, like one-half and two-quarters, they are equivalent.
fifth	When a whole is split into five equal parts it is called a fifth. One-fifth is written $\frac{1}{5}$, two-fifths is written $\frac{2}{5}$ and so on.
fraction	A part of a whole written with one number above another is called a fraction.
half	When a whole is split into two equal parts each part is called a half. One-half is written $\frac{1}{2}$.
halve	When we split a whole into two equal parts we halve it.
mixed number	A whole number and a fraction with the total value greater than one whole, such as one and one-quarter, is called a mixed number.
numerator	The number on the top of a fraction is called the numerator. It shows how many equal parts are being described.
quarter	When a whole is split into four equal parts each part is called a quarter. One-quarter is written $\frac{1}{4}$, two-quarters is written $\frac{2}{4}$ and three-quarters is written $\frac{3}{4}$.
tenth	When a whole is split into ten equal parts each part is called a tenth. One-tenth is written $\frac{1}{10}$ or as the decimal 0.1, two-tenths is written $\frac{2}{10}$ or as the decimal 0.2 and so on.
third	When a whole is split into three equal parts each part is called a third. One-third is written $\frac{1}{3}$ and two-thirds is written $\frac{2}{3}$.
unit fraction	A fraction with the numerator 1 is called a unit fraction.

Schofield&Sims

the long-established educational publisher specialising in maths, English and science

Schofield & Sims Fractions, Decimals and Percentages is a whole-school programme that supports a mastery approach to teaching and learning this tricky area of maths. Comprising six pupil books and six accompanying teacher's guides, this structured series helps pupils to develop a deep, secure and adaptable understanding of fractions, building up to decimals, percentages, ratio and proportion. Through engaging lessons and rich practice questions, pupils encounter these topics in a broad range of contexts and representations to encourage mathematical fluency.

Each pupil book provides:
- full curriculum coverage
- a user-friendly summary of the key learning point of each unit
- plenty of practice, from quick questions that help pupils gain confidence to more challenging problems that build conceptual understanding and reasoning skills
- regular revision tests to reinforce learning and identify strengths and weaknesses
- a self-evaluation checklist that encourages pupils to assess their own learning
- a glossary to expand mathematical vocabulary.

The accompanying teacher's guides contain lesson plans, answers to all the questions in the pupil book, and assessment and record-keeping resources. A selection of free downloads is also available.

Fractions 3 supports the National Curriculum requirements for Year 3 and covers the following topic areas: using unit and non-unit fractions; comparing and ordering fractions with the same denominator; finding equivalent fractions using a fraction wall; counting in tenths; adding and subtracting fractions with the same denominator; and problem solving.

Fractions 1	ISBN 978 07217 1375 5	**Fractions 1 Teacher's Guide**	ISBN 978 07217 1376 2
Fractions 2	ISBN 978 07217 1377 9	**Fractions 2 Teacher's Guide**	ISBN 978 07217 1378 6
Fractions 3	ISBN 978 07217 1379 3	**Fractions 3 Teacher's Guide**	ISBN 978 07217 1380 9
Fractions 4	ISBN 978 07217 1381 6	**Fractions 4 Teacher's Guide**	ISBN 978 07217 1382 3
Fractions 5	ISBN 978 07217 1383 0	**Fractions 5 Teacher's Guide**	ISBN 978 07217 1384 7
Fractions 6	ISBN 978 07217 1385 4	**Fractions 6 Teacher's Guide**	ISBN 978 07217 1386 1

For online answers and supporting downloads, scan the QR code or visit www.schofieldandsims.co.uk/free-downloads

MIX
Paper | Supporting responsible forestry
FSC® C023114

For further information and to place your order visit www.schofieldandsims.co.uk or telephone 01484 607080

ISBN 978 07217 1379 3
Key Stage 2
Age range 7–8 years
£4.95 (Retail price)

ISBN 978 07217 1379 3